Robby in the River

Written by Judy Waite

Illustrated by Judy Brown

Lucy and Dad took Robby for a walk by the river.
Lucy and Robby ran down
the muddy path.

Robby liked to fetch things.

He fetched
an old boot
for Lucy.

He fetched
some smelly
weed.

He tried to fetch
a big branch.

"No, Robby, that's too big," said Lucy. "Fetch this little stick instead," she called.

Robby liked fetching the stick.
He fetched it again...

...and again...

...and again.

Suddenly, Lucy slipped
on the muddy path.
"Whoops!"
She fell down and the stick
went into the river.

Robby ran after the stick.

"No!" shouted Lucy and Dad.

But it was too late.

Splash!

Robby jumped into the river.

Lucy and Dad looked down.
Robby was swimming round
and round.
He couldn't get out.

"I know," said Lucy. "I'll get
that big branch."
"Yes," said Dad. "Quick!"
Lucy got the branch and
Dad put it in the river.
"Fetch the branch, Robby," Lucy called.

But Robby didn't seem to hear her.
Lucy was very scared. Robby was
still swimming round and round.

"FETCH IT!" Lucy shouted again.

At last Robby heard her.

He picked up the branch in his teeth,

but the branch slipped into the river.

"Quick, Dad!" said Lucy. "You have to help him."

Dad tried to get the branch.
He almost slipped into the river.
He tried again and at last
he got hold of the branch.
He pulled Robby out of the river.

"What a good thing you got that big branch," said Dad.
"What a good thing Robby saw it in the first place," said Lucy.

Robby shook himself.

He shook water all over Lucy.

Lucy didn't mind.